Beyon

Unravelling JonBenét Ramsey

Beyond the Headlines: Unraveling JonBenét Ramsey

Behind The Mask

Will Anderson

Published by Oliver Lancaster, 2023.

BEYOND THE HEADLINES: UNRAVELING JONBENÉT RAMSEY

First edition. July 8, 2023.

ISBN: 979-8223785569

Written by Will Anderson.

Also by Will Anderson

Behind The Mask
Behind the Mask: Amanda Knox
Behind the Mask: Jeffrey Dahmer
Behind the Mask: Ted Bundy
Behind the Mask: The Devil's Architect H. H. Holmes
Behind the Mask: The Golden State Killer
Behind the Mask: The Zodiac Killer
Beyond the Headlines: The O.J. Simpson Trial
Beyond the Headlines: Unraveling JonBenét Ramsey
Beyond the Headlines: Unraveling the Menendez Brothers

Standalone
The Hatton Garden Heist: Unveiling the Greatest Jewel
Robbery in History

Disclaimer

The information presented in this book, "Beyond the Headlines: Unravelling JonBenét Ramsey," has been thoroughly researched and meticulously gathered from numerous public sources, including newspaper articles, official documents, interview transcripts, and existing literature on the subject. While every effort has been made to ensure the accuracy and reliability of the information, the author acknowledges that some aspects of the case remain disputed or unresolved and that interpretation of the evidence can be subjective.

The views and opinions expressed in this book are those of the author and do not necessarily reflect the official policy or position of any agency involved in the investigation. The author is not a law enforcement officer, forensic expert, or legal professional, and their interpretations of the events and evidence should not be regarded as definitive or authoritative.

This book discusses sensitive topics, including child murder and family tragedy, which some readers may find distressing. The author has made every effort to present these topics with respect, sensitivity, and a deep regard for the victims and those affected by the case.

Lastly, the author and publisher expressly disclaim responsibility for any adverse effects resulting, directly or indirectly, from the information contained in this book.

The purpose of this book is to offer an in-depth exploration of one of the most infamous unsolved cases in American history. It is not intended to accuse or vindicate any individual or group involved in the case. Rather, it is an invitation to engage in an ongoing dialogue about justice, media representation, societal issues, and the enduring mystery of JonBenét Ramsey's tragic death.

Introduction - A Case That Shook the World

———

The story of JonBenét Ramsey, a young beauty queen whose life was tragically cut short, is a chilling narrative that has left a permanent scar on America's consciousness. As mysterious as it is tragic, her unsolved murder in the quiet hours after Christmas 1996, when she was just six years old, became an enduring symbol of a crime that remains, to this day, both shockingly brutal and frustratingly unresolved.

For many, including myself, the discovery of JonBenét's case wasn't through the lenses of personal experience, but rather through the multi-pixelated, high-resolution screen of a television news bulletin, an article in a national newspaper, or, for later generations, a deep-dive into an internet rabbit hole. I remember my own first encounter with the story, a vivid recollection that still stirs a curious combination of empathy, bewilderment, and unquenchable thirst for answers.

I had always been drawn to mysteries, both in fiction and reality, the unsolved puzzles that keep our minds engaged, questioning, and relentlessly pursuing truth. But nothing had quite prepared me for the chilling depths of the JonBenét Ramsey case, the haunting image of a child beauty queen frozen forever at six years old, her blond curls and angelic face obscuring the grim reality of her tragic fate.

It was the duality of JonBenét's life that was particularly striking, a world where childhood innocence was juxtaposed against the high-stakes environment of child pageants. But beyond the glitz and glam, behind the bold headlines, there was a real child, a real family, and a real tragedy that rocked a nation. It was this stark contrast, and the enduring mystery of her untimely death, that captured and held my attention.

Years have passed since I first delved into the abyss of the JonBenét Ramsey case. Yet, it continues to command my curiosity, a strange amalgamation of empathy for a life lost too soon and fascination with the labyrinthine intricacies of a still unsolved crime. It's a story that never fades, a mystery that refuses to be forgotten.

Just like many, I have been gripped by the JonBenét saga, and the more I looked into it, the more complex it seemed. Each piece of evidence, each potential lead, each theory and suspicion only served to deepen the enigma, rather than clarifying it. As such, the case of JonBenét Ramsey, both a media sensation and a haunting crime story, represents a tragic puzzle, pieces of which are missing or simply don't fit together, even after all these years.

So why does this particular case resonate so powerfully? Why, amongst countless other unsolved crimes, does the name JonBenét Ramsey continue to evoke such strong emotions and curiosity? It is these questions, among others, that we will explore in this book.

We will go beyond the headlines, beyond the media circus, and beyond the popular theories to unravel the enigma of JonBenét

Ramsey. We'll examine the known facts, explore the rampant theories, scrutinise the investigation, and question the often overlooked or under-emphasised aspects of the case. In doing so, we hope to breathe new life into the quest for answers, keeping alive the memory of a little girl lost, and reminding us that behind every headline, there is a story, a tragedy, and a truth waiting to be uncovered.

A Labyrinth of Uncertainties - The Unanswered Questions of the JonBenét Ramsey Case

IN THE WORLD OF CRIME-solving and mystery-debunking, unanswered questions form the very crux of our curiosity, our intrigue, and our ceaseless quest for justice. It is these mysteries, the questions left hanging in the cold Boulder air, that make the JonBenét Ramsey case such an enduring enigma. From the lack of a definitive suspect to the cryptic ransom note left behind, each unanswered question adds a new layer of complexity to an already convoluted case.

Here, I will delve into three of the most compelling questions that I, and undoubtedly many others, have about the JonBenét Ramsey case - questions that continue to perplex, fascinate, and challenge our understanding of the case even after all these years.

1. Who wrote the ransom note?

ONE OF THE MOST BAFFLING pieces of evidence in the JonBenét case is undoubtedly the ransom note. Left on the kitchen staircase by the supposed kidnapper, this three-page note, with its strange language and peculiarities, sparked more questions than answers. Who was the author of this note? The handwriting was never conclusively matched to anyone in the Ramsey family or any suspects. Moreover, the note requested a peculiarly specific ransom amount, identical to John Ramsey's bonus that year. It remains a strange, unexplained piece of evidence that fuels the enduring mystery of JonBenét's murder.

2. How did the murder take place inside a busy family home undetected?

ON THE NIGHT OF THE murder, the Ramsey home was anything but deserted. JonBenét's parents, Patsy and John, her brother, Burke, were all home, yet no one claimed to have heard anything unusual during the night. The question remains: How was it possible for a murder, which evidence suggests involved a struggle, to take place inside a bustling family home, without anyone hearing or seeing anything?

3. Why were the crime scene and the investigation so mishandled?

MANY CLAIM THAT ONE of the main reasons the JonBenét case remains unsolved is the initial mishandling of the crime scene. Family friends were allowed to clean areas of the house, potentially contaminating the crime scene, and the police failed to secure JonBenét's room. The body was also moved by John Ramsey before forensic experts could analyse the scene. These missteps undoubtedly complicated the case, and it leads us to question: What vital pieces of evidence were missed or contaminated due to this mishandling?

Each of these questions, unresolved and haunting, encapsulates the enigmatic nature of the JonBenét Ramsey case. They represent the endless threads of this intricate tapestry, each leading us down a different path in our search for truth. But perhaps it is in these unanswered questions, these persistent unknowns, that we can begin to unravel the enduring mystery of JonBenét Ramsey

Cultural Impact of the JonBenét Ramsey Case

IN THE VAST EXPANSE of unsolved mysteries and high-profile crime cases, a handful carve their place deeply into the public psyche, living on beyond their moment, extending their grip across generations. The JonBenét Ramsey case is undeniably one of those. Despite the passage of years and the ebb and flow of countless other headlines, it continues to captivate, to haunt, and to stir a public fascination that seems impervious to time. But why? What is it about this particular case that holds our collective interest captive?

One explanation lies in the very heart of human nature: our fascination with dichotomy, with contrasts and contradictions. The case of JonBenét Ramsey presents a stark dichotomy that's both enthralling and unsettling. A little girl living in the opulent world of beauty pageants, radiating charisma and talent well beyond her tender years, meets a cruel and inconceivably brutal end in her own home. This incongruity between the exuberant brightness of JonBenét's life and the darkness of her death is a chilling juxtaposition that continues to fascinate and perplex.

Moreover, the unsolved nature of the case is a critical element in its enduring appeal. Human beings are instinctively drawn to mysteries, our minds tirelessly seeking patterns, solutions, and closure. The JonBenét case, with its tangled web of unanswered questions, unconfirmed suspects, and unresolved issues, provides an intricate puzzle that invites constant examination, speculation, and debate.

Perhaps, though, the most profound reason why the JonBenét Ramsey case continues to captivate is its deep resonance with societal issues and enduring cultural narratives. JonBenét, a child thrust into the adult world of beauty pageants, has become a symbol of our society's problematic relationship with child fame and the sexualization of young girls. The heated debate surrounding child beauty pageants, their implications on a child's mental health and identity, became particularly intense in the wake of JonBenét's death, her image raising uncomfortable questions about innocence lost too soon.

Simultaneously, the Ramsey case serves as a mirror reflecting the flaws in our criminal justice system. The perceived mishandling of the case by the Boulder Police Department has led to public outcry and ongoing debates about law enforcement's competence, biases, and overall effectiveness.

Finally, the extensive media coverage of JonBenét's case has been both a mirror and a moulder of public opinion. The case was one of the first to play out in the age of 24-hour news cycles, internet sleuthing, and the court of public opinion. The images of JonBenét, the speculative theories, and the portrayal of the

Ramsey family shaped public discourse and brought attention to the power and ethical responsibilities of media.

The JonBenét Ramsey case, therefore, is more than an unsolved murder; it's a cultural touchstone, a societal reflection, and a cautionary tale. It continues to resonate, capturing our collective interest, forcing us to question, to confront, and to remember. As we delve further into the complexities of this case, it is important to consider these broader cultural implications and the way they color our understanding and perception of JonBenét Ramsey's tragic story.

A Personal Journey - The Motivation Behind the Mystery

THE PURSUIT OF UNSOLVED mysteries is a journey that can feel both immensely personal and strikingly universal. On the one hand, we are driven by our own curiosity, our need for understanding, our desire to make sense of the inexplicable. On the other hand, we find ourselves part of a larger collective, sharing our questions, theories, and discoveries with a community united by a common fascination.

My personal journey into the heart of the JonBenét Ramsey case was initially sparked by a combination of interest in criminology and a profound sense of empathy for a young life cut tragically short. The dichotomous image of JonBenét - a child beauty queen who became the victim of a horrific crime - was a haunting portrait that seemed to demand exploration.

Delving into the case, I was struck by the number of unanswered questions, the inconsistencies, and the various theories that emerged from every corner. Each revealed a different aspect of the story, but none provided a clear resolution. As I moved deeper into the labyrinth of the case, my motivation evolved from a personal quest to a broader mission. I felt compelled to share my exploration, to bring others along on the journey, and to contribute to the collective effort to unravel this enduring enigma.

With this book, "Beyond the Headlines: Unravelling JonBenét Ramsey," my primary aim is to offer a comprehensive, balanced, and thoughtful examination of the case. This is not about positing a definitive solution or pinning blame on one individual or theory. Instead, it is about laying out the known facts, assessing the credibility of various theories, and critically evaluating the investigative process.

Moreover, I seek to humanise JonBenét, to move beyond the sensational headlines and the infamous images of the child beauty queen, and to remember the young girl whose life was taken too soon. Amid the media frenzy and the swirl of theories, it is all too easy to forget that at the centre of this mystery was a real child with a life full of potential, a family left grappling with a heartbreaking loss, and a community shaken to its core.

Finally, I hope this book will inspire critical thinking and encourage informed discussion about the case. By presenting a balanced account, I aim to provide readers with a foundation upon which they can draw their own conclusions, ask their own questions, and continue their own exploration of this complex case.

In the end, the quest to unravel the mystery of JonBenét Ramsey is more than a search for the identity of a perpetrator; it is a journey toward understanding, empathy, and ultimately, justice for a little girl who will forever remain in the heart of public consciousness.

The Path Ahead - A Guide Through the Mystery

THE STRUCTURE OF A book serves as a roadmap for readers, charting a course through the labyrinth of information, ideas, and perspectives. In "Beyond the Headlines: Unravelling JonBenét Ramsey," I have carefully considered the organisation of chapters to provide a comprehensive, logical, and thoughtful exploration of this complex case.

Each chapter in the forthcoming sections of the book is designed to delve into a specific aspect of the case, layering information and analysis to create a holistic understanding of the mystery surrounding JonBenét's death. We'll venture beyond the headlines, navigating through the infamous ransom note, the perplexing crime scene, the role of the media, the various suspects and theories, and the broader societal implications of the case.

The aspect of the case I am particularly eager to delve into is the societal and cultural implications of JonBenét's story. How did society react to the death of a child beauty queen? How did the media shape public perception and discourse? And what does this case reveal about our understanding of child fame, law enforcement, and justice?

This book is not about rushing to conclusions or sensationalising a tragedy. Instead, it is about undertaking a thoughtful, comprehensive exploration of a case that has captivated public consciousness for decades. As we progress through the chapters, my hope is to shed light on the many facets of the case, fostering a deeper understanding of the enduring mystery of JonBenét Ramsey.

Treading Lightly - The Ethical Implications of Unravelling JonBenét Ramsey

WRITING ABOUT A REAL-life tragedy, especially one involving a child's death, is not an endeavour to be undertaken lightly. It requires a delicate balance between curiosity and respect, analysis and empathy, exposure and privacy. This is particularly true for a case like JonBenét Ramsey's, which is steeped in public intrigue and media sensationalism. As we venture further into this exploration, it's crucial to acknowledge the sensitivity surrounding the case and its potential impact on the Ramsey family and others involved.

One of the fundamental ethical considerations when delving into such a sensitive case is respect for the people involved, primarily JonBenét and her family. Behind the headlines, theories, and speculation lie real individuals who experienced an unimaginable loss. Throughout this book, I aim to honour JonBenét's memory and maintain respect for her family's grief, ensuring their experiences are not reduced to mere fodder for intrigue or sensationalism.

Furthermore, it's important to recognize that while we strive to unravel the mysteries surrounding JonBenét's case, we must also respect the limits of our knowledge. We have access to information made public through police records, media reports, and published accounts of those involved, but we don't have the complete picture. Thus, any conclusions drawn or theories postulated should be presented with caution and clearly framed as interpretations based on available information rather than definitive truths.

In discussing potential suspects or theories, it's essential to maintain fairness and to avoid perpetuating unsubstantiated rumours or defamatory statements. The ethical responsibility here is twofold: to ensure accuracy and fairness in presenting information and to avoid causing undue harm to individuals who have been under suspicion.

A key aspect of responsible exploration is the critical examination of the role the media has played in the case. The media's portrayal of JonBenét, her family, and the investigation has greatly influenced public perception of the case. Thus, we need to scrutinise media narratives and question how they may have shaped our understanding of the case, being mindful of potential bias, sensationalism, or misinformation.

Finally, considering the emotional toll this case can take on readers, I am committed to discussing the grisly details of JonBenét's murder with utmost sensitivity. While it's necessary to provide enough information to understand the case, gratuitous descriptions or graphic details that serve no analytical purpose will be avoided.

In "Beyond the Headlines: Unravelling JonBenét Ramsey," the commitment to ethical and sensitive exploration is paramount. This is not just a mystery to be solved; it's a young girl's life and legacy to be respected, a family's grief to be acknowledged, and a societal reflection to be handled with care.

An Invitation - Joining the Journey of Discovery

UNRAVELLING A MYSTERY is not a solitary endeavour; it's a shared voyage of discovery, a collective endeavour to piece together an intricate puzzle. As we stand at the precipice of this journey into the heart of the JonBenét Ramsey case, I invite you, the readers, to not just passively absorb information, but actively participate in the exploration and discussion.

In writing "Beyond the Headlines: Unravelling JonBenét Ramsey," I hope to provide more than a recounting of events or an exposition of theories. I aim to facilitate an interactive experience, inviting you to scrutinise the evidence, challenge the theories, ask your own questions, and form your own perspectives.

Each chapter is intended as a conversation starter, a catalyst for your own exploration. As we dissect the events of that fateful night, analyse the perplexing ransom note, evaluate the evidence, and consider the societal implications, I encourage you to not just accept but question, not just read but ponder. Engage with the material, debate the ideas, and consider the broader implications of the case on our society and our understanding of justice.

I hope that this book will stimulate thoughtful discussion, critical thinking, and a deeper understanding of the complexities surrounding JonBenét's case. It is my sincere hope that through this interactive journey, we can shed light on a story that has been steeped in speculation and uncertainty.

However, as we embark on this expedition, I urge you to remember the sensitivity of the subject matter. This isn't a fictional story; it's a tragic reality that affected real people. In our quest for understanding, we must maintain a respectful and empathetic approach, ensuring our discussion honours the memory of JonBenét and respects those whose lives were irrevocably altered by this tragedy.

So, dear readers, as we delve into the intricate layers of the JonBenét Ramsey case, I welcome you to this collective journey. Bring your curiosity, your insights, your empathy, and your respect. Together, let's venture beyond the headlines, toward a deeper understanding of one of the most enduring mysteries of our time.

Chapter 1: A Perfect Christmas, A Haunting Disappearance

Under the Christmas Lights - The Ramsey Family

The Ramsey family, at first glance, epitomised the quintessential American dream. John Bennett Ramsey, a successful businessman, and Patricia 'Patsy' Ramsey, a former beauty queen, along with their two children, Burke and JonBenét, were a picture of prosperity and happiness nestled in the upscale neighbourhood of Boulder, Colorado.

John, a successful entrepreneur, had built a multimillion-dollar business, Access Graphics, while Patsy, a former Miss West Virginia, brought her beauty pageant grace into the home, instilling a sense of style, elegance, and ambition within her children. Burke, nine years older than JonBenét, seemed to live a typical life of a young boy, while JonBenét, with her radiant smile and captivating charm, followed in her mother's footsteps, making her mark in child beauty pageants.

Their home, a sprawling Tudor-style mansion at 755 15th Street, was a beacon of grandeur and affluence, but beyond the façade of prosperity, it was filled with the warm, vibrant energy of a family deeply connected to their traditions, particularly around Christmas.

The Christmas season for the Ramsey family was more than just a holiday; it was a grand celebration filled with love, laughter, and an array of treasured family traditions. The Ramsey household would transform into a festive wonderland, echoing with the sound of Christmas carols and the rich aroma of baked cookies, a magical setting that would make any child's eyes sparkle with excitement.

The house would be adorned with sparkling lights and garlands, a towering Christmas tree taking the place of pride in the living room, its branches laden with ornaments collected over the years, each telling a story of its own. Handcrafted decorations made by the children added a personal touch, showcasing their creativity and their joyous anticipation of the holiday.

The festivities would include an annual Christmas party hosted by the Ramseys, where friends and neighbours would come together to celebrate the season. These gatherings, filled with cheerful conversations, gift exchanges, and shared meals, highlighted the Ramseys' prominent place within their community and their penchant for hosting and celebrating.

Among these traditions, a particularly cherished one was the family's annual visit to the local church on Christmas Eve, followed by Patsy reading Christmas stories to JonBenét and Burke. Each Christmas morning, the children would wake up to find gifts from Santa Claus under the tree, their excited squeals filling the house with joyous energy.

These idyllic Christmas celebrations offered a glimpse into the life of the Ramsey family - a life that, to the outside observer, appeared filled with love, prosperity, and happiness. However, this picture-perfect scene would be forever marred by the tragic events that unfolded on December 26, 1996, casting a long, unshakeable shadow over the Ramsey household.

The Day of the Incident - December 25, 1996

AS WE VENTURE INTO the heart of the mystery surrounding JonBenét Ramsey's tragic death, it's essential to create a detailed picture of the day leading up to her disappearance - Christmas Day, 1996.

Christmas morning began as any other for the Ramsey family. In line with their annual tradition, the children, Burke and JonBenét, woke up to find gifts from Santa Claus under the tree. Their excited laughter echoed through the house, filling the air with a palpable sense of joy and celebration. It was a scene of idyllic domestic bliss, a family ensconced in the warmth of their Christmas celebrations, completely unaware of the horror that would soon unfold.

The day continued with a quiet family lunch at home, filled with traditional holiday fare. As per accounts, the mood was light, the atmosphere joyful. In the afternoon, JonBenét and her older brother, Burke, played with their new Christmas presents while John and Patsy attended to the final preparations for their planned trip to Michigan, which was scheduled for the next day.

Later in the evening, the family attended a dinner at the home of their friends, Fleet and Priscilla White. The party was cheerful and lively, with JonBenét reportedly in high spirits, engaging enthusiastically with the other children present. The Ramseys returned home around 10 p.m., and according to Patsy, she helped JonBenét change into her pyjamas and put her to bed.

The family's activities on that day seemed relatively ordinary, with no overt signs of anything unusual or foreboding. However, certain events have been highlighted by investigators and theorists as potentially significant.

Firstly, during the day, Burke had reportedly received a model aeroplane as a gift, a fact that some have linked to a peculiar detail found at the crime scene - a piece of the model track was allegedly used in the garrote found on JonBenét's body. While this connection remains speculative, it's one of the many threads of this case that have fueled debate and speculation.

Additionally, a neighbour reportedly saw an unfamiliar car parked across the street from the Ramsey house on the afternoon of Christmas Day. While this observation might seem innocuous, in the context of the case, it's been subject to intense scrutiny.

Finally, and perhaps most ominously, a 911 call was allegedly made from the Ramsey house around 5:30 p.m., but was quickly terminated. The Boulder Police received the call but dismissed it as a mistake due to the lack of voice contact. This event has been considered a potential red flag by some investigators, though its significance remains a point of contention.

December 25, 1996, started as a day of celebration for the Ramsey family but ended as the prologue to a nightmare that would last for decades. As we delve further into the events of that fateful night, each of these details, no matter how minor they seem, could hold the key to unravelling the mystery of JonBenét's tragic end.

WILL ANDERSON

Chapter 2: A Media Storm: The Public's Obsession

―――――

Through the Lens of the Media - Coverage and Consequences

The role of the media in the JonBenét Ramsey case cannot be underestimated. From the initial reaction to her disappearance to the subsequent saturation of coverage, the media played a significant part in shaping public perception, steering conversations, and in many ways, fueling speculation and mystery around the case.

The initial reaction to JonBenét's disappearance was shock and disbelief. Here was a six-year-old beauty queen from an affluent family in an idyllic community, found murdered in her own home the day after Christmas. The circumstances were chilling, and the media quickly latched onto the story, drawn to its tragic and sensational elements.

Local news outlets were the first to cover the case, and their reports were picked up by national media soon after. The story of JonBenét's murder was splashed across television screens, newspapers, and magazines. Every development, no matter how minute, was reported and analysed, creating a constant stream of coverage that catapulted the case into the national consciousness.

However, as time passed, the media coverage shifted from straightforward reporting to intense speculation. With the lack of concrete answers from the police, the media began presenting theories and hypotheses about what might have happened. Many outlets leaned into the sensational aspects of the case, focusing on the family's wealth, Patsy's involvement in the child beauty pageant circuit, and the peculiar details of the murder.

The Ramseys, who had initially been seen as victims, found themselves at the centre of suspicion. This was fueled in part by their initial reluctance to engage with the media and law enforcement, a decision that, though guided by their attorney, created an image of secrecy that the media capitalised on. Their eventual press appearances did little to quell the speculation; if anything, they added more fuel to the fire.

The media's portrayal of JonBenét was another contentious point. She was often depicted in her pageant attire, wearing makeup and striking adult-like poses. These images, often taken out of context, painted an uncomfortable picture, serving to sensationalise the case further and sparking debates about child exploitation and the sexualization of young girls.

The saturation of media coverage around the case inevitably shaped public opinion. The mystery of JonBenét's murder was no longer a mere crime story; it became a national obsession, a real-life whodunit unfolding in real-time. The media, in its pursuit of headlines, often blurred the lines between fact and fiction, objective reporting and sensationalism.

While the media's role in highlighting the case was crucial, it's worth questioning whether the relentless coverage and speculation helped or hindered the pursuit of justice for JonBenét. As we continue to delve deeper into the case, it's vital to separate the facts from the speculation, the reality from the media's portrayal, in our quest for truth.

The Rise of the Armchair Detective - Public Fascination with the Ramsey Case

THE JONBENÉT RAMSEY case not only captured the attention of the public but also gave rise to an unexpected phenomenon – the emergence of armchair detectives and the intensification of public fascination with true crime. This was a case that seemed made for amateur sleuthing, with its myriad of unanswered questions, its unusual pieces of evidence, and its seemingly perfect family enveloped in a tragic mystery.

From the moment the case made headlines, it spurred an outpouring of public engagement. People across America, and indeed the world, were riveted by the shocking details and the baffling complexities of the case. The mysterious ransom note, the odd circumstances of the discovery of JonBenét's body, the incongruities in the parents' accounts - all these served as fuel for speculation and debate.

But this was more than just an armchair interest; people started actively participating in the investigation, albeit from the comfort of their living rooms. With the wealth of information available through media coverage, online forums, and later, documentary series, anyone with an internet connection and an interest in the case could play detective.

These amateur sleuths painstakingly dissected every detail, proposed theories, and engaged in intense debates in online forums. They analysed the 911 call made by Patsy, dissected the ransom note word for word, and speculated on the significance of the pineapple found in JonBenét's stomach during her autopsy. From passionate hobbyists to dedicated online communities, the public dove headfirst into the investigative fray.

This phenomenon undoubtedly underscored a broader societal trend – the public's growing fascination with true crime. The JonBenét case became a kind of cultural touchstone for this movement, epitomising the allure of the unsolved and the unknown. It illustrated our collective curiosity about the darker aspects of human nature and our eagerness to untangle the complexities of crime from a safe distance.

Yet, while this active engagement underscores an inherent desire for justice and truth, it also raises important questions. How reliable are these amateur investigations? Can public speculation muddy the waters and distract from the factual evidence? Do they contribute to, or detract from, the pursuit of justice?

In the quest to unravel the JonBenét Ramsey mystery, these armchair detectives have emerged as a significant force, contributing to the enduring fascination with the case. As we continue to navigate this complex narrative, their role, influence, and the broader implications of this amateur sleuthing phenomenon will serve as a compelling thread in the fabric of this story.

WILL ANDERSON

Chapter 3: The Suspects: Shadows in the Spotlight

―――――

Shadows of Doubt - The Ramseys Under Scrutiny

The tragic tale of JonBenét Ramsey inevitably saw suspicion fall on those closest to her - her parents, John and Patsy Ramsey. Despite their pleas of innocence and their grief over the loss of their daughter, several factors raised eyebrows and led investigators and the public to consider them as potential suspects.

The first suspicious element was the ransom note found by Patsy. The note was unusually long, written on a pad of paper from the Ramsey home, and the practice drafts were found at the scene. The demand for $118,000, nearly the same amount as John's recent bonus, further intensified suspicions. Many experts found the language in the note to be theatrical and unlike typical kidnapping demands. Handwriting analysts also pointed out similarities between Patsy's writing and the note, although no definitive conclusions were reached.

The peculiar circumstances surrounding the discovery of JonBenét's body also raised questions. Hours after reporting her abduction, John found JonBenét's body in a little-used part of the basement, an area police had already searched. The fact that John disturbed the crime scene by moving JonBenét's body also drew suspicion, despite it being an understandable reaction for a grieving parent.

The inconsistencies in the Ramseys' accounts of what transpired that morning furthered doubts. Differences in their recounting of events such as when they last saw JonBenét, whether they checked on her before going to bed, or if the house was locked up, became focal points for scrutiny.

The Ramsey's behaviour following the tragedy also drew critical attention. Their initial refusal to speak to police separately, their hiring of defence attorneys, and their limited cooperation with law enforcement were seen as unusual for grieving parents. However, it's important to consider the immense pressure and suspicion they were under, which might have necessitated such measures for self-protection.

Finally, the fact that JonBenét was killed in the supposed safety of her own home raised questions about who might have had access and motive. The lack of evidence of forced entry suggested familiarity with the house, further implicating the parents in the eyes of the public.

While all these factors painted a picture of suspicion around the Ramseys, it's important to remember that they were never formally charged with a crime related to JonBenét's death. In 2008, new DNA testing cleared them and their son Burke of any involvement in the crime. Yet, the cloud of suspicion that hung over them for so long illustrates the complexity and intrigue that has come to define the JonBenét Ramsey case.

The examination of John and Patsy Ramsey's role, or lack thereof, in this tragedy offers insight into the intricate, often fraught process of seeking truth amidst tragedy, grief, and public scrutiny.

Other Shadows - The Intruder Theories

DESPITE THE SUSPICION that surrounded the Ramseys, several compelling theories propose that JonBenét's murder was the work of an intruder. The presence of unknown male DNA found on JonBenét's underwear and long johns, the unidentified boot print in the basement, and the mysterious broken window have all pointed investigators and armchair detectives toward the possibility of an outsider involved in the crime.

One of the earliest intruder theories pointed to a local man who played Santa Claus in the community. Bill McReynolds, who had given JonBenét a card saying she would receive a "special gift" after Christmas, was looked into but eventually cleared by the police. His peculiar connection to JonBenét, however, sparked speculation and left an indelible mark on public consciousness.

Another person of interest was Michael Helgoth, a local junkyard owner. Helgoth owned a pair of boots that allegedly matched the unidentified print found at the crime scene. Moreover, he had a stun gun, which some believe could explain the two mysterious marks on JonBenét's body. Helgoth died by suicide shortly after JonBenét's death, leading some to speculate about his potential involvement, although no concrete evidence has ever linked him to the crime.

Perhaps the most widely discussed intruder theory is the "ransom kidnapper" theory. Supporters of this theory point to the unusual ransom note demanding a specific sum of money as evidence of a kidnapping attempt gone wrong. They argue that the perpetrator broke into the house while the Ramseys were out, wrote the ransom note, and then killed JonBenét in a panic when she woke up.

The more sinister theory of a sex offender targeting JonBenét also gained traction, supported by the disturbing evidence of sexual assault. The beauty pageants JonBenét participated in, often broadcasted on local television, might have drawn the attention of predators, making this theory chillingly plausible.

However, all these theories grapple with the absence of clear signs of forced entry. While there was a broken basement window, it was unclear if it was broken at the time of the murder or earlier. Additionally, the intricate layout of the house suggests the intruder would need to have intimate knowledge of the premises.

The multitude of intruder theories, while lacking definitive evidence, underscore the enduring mystery surrounding JonBenét's murder. Each theory carries its own set of compelling arguments and problematic inconsistencies, mirroring the broader complexity of the case itself. As we explore these possibilities, it's crucial to approach them with an open yet critical mind, ever aware of the high stakes in our quest for the truth.

Chapter 4: The Intricate Web: Clues and Contradictions

———

Behind Closed Doors - The Crime Scene and Its Clues

The Ramsey home, a sprawling Tudor-style mansion in the heart of Boulder, Colorado, was transformed from a site of familial warmth and Christmas cheer into a chilling crime scene on the morning of December 26, 1996. It was here, in this seemingly secure and serene setting, that the brutal murder of JonBenét Ramsey took place. This chapter aims to paint a detailed picture of the crime scene, highlighting key elements and notable discrepancies that continue to confound investigators and observers alike.

The morning unfolded with Patsy's discovery of a ransom note on the stairs leading to the kitchen, setting the stage for the dreadful revelations to come. The note, a three-page long narrative demanding exactly $118,000 for JonBenét's safe return, was written using a pen and paper from the Ramsey house itself. This detail suggested that the writer had spent considerable time within the house, a factor that sowed the seeds of doubt and debate.

A thorough search of the house initially failed to reveal any trace of JonBenét. However, later that day, John made the grisly discovery of JonBenét's body in a little-used part of the basement, known as the wine cellar. She was found with a garrote made from a length of cord and a broken paintbrush from Patsy's hobby kit around her neck, her wrists tied above her head, and her mouth covered with duct tape. Notably, a blanket from a nearby room was wrapped around her, a seemingly incongruous act of care in the midst of such violence.

The autopsy report added further layers to the enigma. JonBenét had been hit on the head, strangled, and there was evidence of sexual assault. Intriguingly, undigested pineapple was found in her stomach, although neither John nor Patsy remembered her eating pineapple before bed. This discrepancy prompted speculation about the timeline of events and JonBenét's interactions prior to her death.

Further inspection of the house revealed a broken basement window and an unidentified boot print in the cellar. Despite these potential signs of an intruder, there was no definitive evidence of forced entry. The house, with its numerous entrances and labyrinthine layout, presented a challenge for investigators, adding to the confusion and complexity of the case.

The crime scene, with its bewildering mix of clues, has been the subject of endless scrutiny and speculation. Each piece of evidence seems to open up new questions and avenues of inquiry, from the strangely specific ransom note to the undigested pineapple in JonBenét's stomach. As we delve deeper into these enigmatic details, we strive to piece together a coherent narrative from a puzzle that has vexed investigators for decades.

Deciphering the Ransom Demand

AMONG THE CONFOUNDING pieces of evidence left behind in the JonBenét Ramsey case, the ransom note stands out as one of the most puzzling. It is an anomaly not only for its length and detail but also for its intimate connection to the Ramsey home. The content, handwriting analysis, and theories surrounding the note form a complex web of intrigue that we aim to unravel in this chapter.

The ransom note, discovered on the kitchen staircase by Patsy Ramsey, was written on a pad from the Ramsey home using a Sharpie pen also from the house. Strikingly, it spanned nearly three pages, an extraordinary length for a ransom demand. In the world of crime, ransom notes tend to be brief and to the point, minimising the chance of the writer being identified. Yet, this note was verbose and oddly dramatic, almost as if it were lifted from a crime novel.

Its content added further layers to the mystery. The demand for $118,000 was peculiarly precise and nearly matched John Ramsey's bonus that year, an obscure detail that few outside the family would be privy to. It also contained an unusual sign-off, "Victory! S.B.T.C," the meaning of which remains a subject of intense speculation.

The note sparked myriad theories and extensive handwriting analysis. Initial analysis by the Colorado Bureau of Investigation reported that Patsy Ramsey, despite certain similarities, was not an exact match. However, later analysis by independent experts disagreed, claiming that there were striking resemblances between Patsy's handwriting and that in the note. Despite these analyses, the question of authorship remains inconclusive, with no charges ever brought.

Several theories have emerged concerning the note. The Intruder Theory suggests that an outsider penned it while the Ramseys were at a Christmas party, using it as a misdirection. In contrast, the Ramsey Theory posits that one of the Ramseys wrote the note in a panic after JonBenét's death, attempting to stage a kidnapping to divert suspicion.

The ransom note, with its striking anomalies and ambiguous origins, continues to be a focal point in the Ramsey case. It remains one of the most perplexing and controversial pieces of evidence, encapsulating the enduring enigma that is the JonBenét Ramsey case. As we scrutinise its contents, debate its authorship, and explore its various theories, we inch ever closer to the heart of this unfathomable mystery.

BEYOND THE HEADLINES: UNRAVELING JONBENÉT RAMSEY

Chapter 5: The Unravelling: Police Investigation and Missteps

────

Boulder Police and the Early Investigation

The initial response of the Boulder Police Department to the JonBenét Ramsey case has been a subject of controversy and debate for decades. The early hours of an investigation can often make or break a case, and for the police in Boulder, the JonBenét case was a formidable challenge, fraught with a myriad of complex issues and potential missteps.

The first challenge came in the form of the crime scene itself. As previously discussed, the Ramsey home was large and labyrinthine, presenting a formidable task for investigators. Furthermore, due to the initial report of a kidnapping, the house was not immediately sealed off as a potential crime scene. This led to contamination of evidence as friends, family, and support personnel freely moved through the home.

Another controversial aspect of the case is the fact that the police did not immediately separate and interview John and Patsy Ramsey. In typical investigations, immediate family members are usually interviewed separately as soon as possible to maintain the integrity of their individual accounts. However, this was not done in the case of the Ramseys, and the couple were not formally interviewed until four months after JonBenét's death.

The ransom note, arguably one of the most critical pieces of evidence, also presented difficulties. The decision to hand over the original note to the Ramseys for a television appearance before making a photocopy is widely considered a mistake. The note was handled by multiple individuals, potentially compromising any latent fingerprints or other trace evidence.

The discovery of JonBenét's body by John Ramsey also presented a significant challenge. Instead of preserving the crime scene, John picked up his daughter's body and carried her upstairs, inadvertently tampering with the crime scene. It's an understandable reaction for a grieving father, yet it undoubtedly complicated the ongoing investigation.

The police faced additional criticism for their lack of experience in dealing with such high-profile cases. The Boulder Police Department had not handled a murder case for several years, and their relative inexperience was exploited by a savvy defence team hired by the Ramseys.

All of these challenges contributed to a sense of confusion and inefficiency in the early days of the investigation. While it's easy to cast blame in hindsight, it's important to consider the immense pressure and unprecedented nature of the case the Boulder Police were dealing with. The early stages of the JonBenét Ramsey investigation, with its potential missteps and challenges, remain a critical point of consideration in our ongoing exploration of this enduring mystery.

Missteps in Blue - Law Enforcement Controversies

THE JONBENÉT RAMSEY case brought to light several controversial decisions made by the Boulder Police Department that have since raised questions about the integrity of the investigation. Each decision, whether it involved mishandled evidence, miscommunication, or faulty interrogation techniques, undeniably left an imprint on the course of the investigation and its ultimate outcomes.

One of the most significant controversies involved the handling of the crime scene. When JonBenét's body was found, John Ramsey carried his daughter upstairs from the basement and laid her on the floor. When the police arrived at the scene, they moved the body again, changing the state of the crime scene multiple times. These actions likely disturbed potential evidence and complicated any subsequent forensic analysis.

Then there was the issue of the ransom note. The police allowed the note to be handled by multiple individuals before it was properly preserved for forensic analysis, possibly contaminating potential fingerprint or DNA evidence. Furthermore, the original note was given to the Ramseys for a television appearance before a photocopy had been made, potentially compromising the document's integrity.

In terms of interrogation, the decision not to immediately separate and interview John and Patsy Ramsey has also been a significant point of contention. Typically, in cases involving a death in a family home, the family members are considered persons of interest and are interviewed separately to ensure the consistency of their statements. This procedure was not followed in the initial stages of the Ramsey case, which has led to criticisms regarding the thoroughness and efficacy of the early investigation.

Another controversy arose when detectives waited for four months to conduct a formal interview with the Ramseys. By this time, the couple had hired a robust legal team, which significantly impacted the way the interrogation process unfolded. This delay is seen by many as a missed opportunity to gather crucial information when memories were still fresh and before the influence of legal counsel.

Each of these decisions, among others, has sparked debate regarding the Boulder Police Department's handling of the JonBenét Ramsey case. While these missteps may appear significant in hindsight, it's important to remember the pressures and complexities inherent in any murder investigation. Nonetheless, understanding these controversies and their potential impact on the investigation is key to our comprehensive exploration of this enduring mystery.

Chapter 6: A Family Divided: The Ramsey's Journey

―――――

In the Spotlight - The Ramseys' Defense and Public Perception

As the JonBenét Ramsey case continued to capture national attention, John and Patsy Ramsey found themselves not only in the midst of an unspeakable tragedy but also at the centre of a media frenzy. With accusations flying and their credibility under siege, the Ramseys undertook numerous media strategies and public appearances to defend their innocence and manage their image. The handling of these efforts and their subsequent impact on the case form the crux of this chapter.

Early in the investigation, the Ramseys, guided by their legal team, adopted a defensive stance. Their initial silence fueled speculation and fed the media's appetite for intrigue. However, this changed on January 1, 1997, when they granted an exclusive interview to CNN. The decision to address the media via a controlled, nationally televised interview rather than speaking directly to local law enforcement was seen as an unconventional and strategic move. While it allowed the Ramseys to assert their innocence and cast doubt on the Boulder Police Department's handling of the case, it also drew criticism and further heightened public interest in the case.

The Ramseys also held press conferences, most notably in May 1997. Patsy Ramsey, visibly distressed, spoke directly to the killer during this conference, stating, "We will find you. We will not be stopped." This public appeal was intended to shift the narrative and refocus attention on the search for JonBenét's killer.

Furthermore, the Ramseys utilised private investigators to conduct parallel investigations, which they used to challenge the official police narrative. They shared these findings with the media, further emphasising their commitment to uncovering the truth and casting themselves in a proactive light.

They also published a book, "The Death of Innocence," in 2000. The book served multiple purposes: it allowed the Ramseys to tell their story in their own words, express their frustration with law enforcement, and share their personal journey of loss and faith. The book was another means to influence public perception and assert their innocence.

The Ramseys' relationship with the media and their efforts to manage their public image were fraught with challenges. While their strategies aimed to defend their innocence and direct attention towards finding the perpetrator, they also faced accusations of being uncooperative with law enforcement and overly controlling of their narrative. These efforts and their impacts continue to be a topic of discussion, demonstrating the pivotal role of media and public perception in high-profile cases like JonBenét Ramsey's.

A Legal Labyrinth - The Ramsey Family's Trials and Tribulations

THE LEGAL JOURNEY OF the Ramsey family is a saga as fraught and enigmatic as the case itself. The tragic loss of JonBenét would become the starting point of a prolonged legal odyssey, teeming with high-stake battles, relentless scrutiny, and immense emotional distress. This chapter will delve into the labyrinthine legal struggles of the Ramseys and the profound impact they bore on their personal lives.

From the onset, the Ramseys faced an onslaught of accusations. Despite no formal charges ever being filed, the spectre of suspicion loomed large. Their every move was scrutinised, both by law enforcement and the public, leading to a considerable strain on their lives. They found themselves engaged in a relentless endeavour to clear their names, navigating a complex legal landscape with tenacity and resilience.

To protect themselves, they hired a formidable team of attorneys and PR professionals who would guide them through the maelstrom. This legal team played a vital role in shaping their defence strategy, challenging law enforcement's narrative, managing their media engagement, and mounting independent investigations. They also fiercely shielded the Ramseys from intrusive media attention and helped them cope with the aggressive accusations that the family faced daily.

However, these battles were not confined to the court of public opinion. In 2000, the Ramseys faced a defamation lawsuit from Chris Wolf, a former suspect in the case, who claimed the couple had implicated him in their book, "The Death of Innocence". After a protracted legal process, the case was dismissed in 2003, providing a semblance of vindication for the beleaguered family.

The emotional toll of these legal ordeals on the Ramseys was palpable. They lived under an unrelenting cloud of suspicion and had to grapple with the fear of potential prosecution. This struggle was exacerbated by their grief over JonBenét's death, making their journey through the legal process even more painful. Their son Burke's life was also significantly impacted as he grew up in the shadow of his sister's unsolved murder, forever marked by the tragedy.

Despite these trials, the Ramseys strived to maintain their faith and unity as a family. They held onto their conviction of innocence, which they maintained until Patsy Ramsey's death in 2006. The legal and emotional challenges they faced remain an integral part of their story and the larger saga of the JonBenét Ramsey case, highlighting the complex intertwining of grief, law, and public scrutiny in high-profile cases.

BEYOND THE HEADLINES: UNRAVELING JONBENÉT RAMSEY

Chapter 7: Justice Delayed: Theories and Speculation

———

The Theoretical Maze - Exploring Hypotheses of the JonBenét Ramsey Case

As with any unresolved case that has captured public fascination, the JonBenét Ramsey murder has given rise to a multitude of theories. Ranging from the plausible to the outright bizarre, these hypotheses have been put forth by law enforcement professionals, expert criminologists, and armchair detectives alike. This chapter will delve into some of these prominent theories, evaluating their strengths, weaknesses, and their role in shaping our understanding of this enigma.

One of the most debated theories is the "Intruder Theory". Supporters of this hypothesis argue that an unknown individual broke into the Ramsey home, possibly with an intent to kidnap JonBenét for ransom, and ended up killing her. The presence of unidentified DNA, an unidentified boot print, and the alleged presence of a suitcase under a window have been touted as evidence. However, detractors point to the lack of signs of forced entry, the oddity of the ransom note, and the fact that JonBenét's body was hidden in a hard-to-find area of the house as contradicting this theory.

On the other end of the spectrum is the "Accidental Death Theory," which posits that JonBenét's death was an accident, perhaps resulting from a blow to the head, and was subsequently covered up by members of her family. The strange circumstances surrounding the ransom note, the strange staging of the crime scene, and the fact that JonBenét was found in her own home all support this theory. However, its critics point to the lack of motive, the inexplicable savagery of the crime if it was indeed an accident, and the steadfast denial of the Ramseys.

Other theories involve scenarios such as a jealous rage by Patsy over bedwetting, Burke's accidental or intentional involvement, or even theories involving Santa Claus impersonators and housekeepers. While some of these theories might seem outlandish, they all attest to the desperation and desire of the public and investigators to find answers in a case where definitive answers seem elusive.

All these theories, each with their own set of strengths and weaknesses, create a complex theoretical tapestry. They highlight the multifaceted nature of the case and the difficulties in reaching a definitive conclusion. As we navigate through this theoretical maze, it's important to keep an open mind, acknowledging that each hypothesis may contain fragments of the elusive truth we seek.

Media Mayhem - Influence on the Investigation and Public Perception

THE MEDIA'S ROLE IN the JonBenét Ramsey case was transformative, to say the least. The unrelenting attention bestowed upon the investigation influenced not only the direction of the case but also significantly shaped public opinion.

BEYOND THE HEADLINES: UNRAVELING JONBENÉT RAMSEY

The exploration of this intricate relationship between the media, the investigation, and public perception forms the essence of this chapter.

One of the initial instances where media coverage steered the case's direction was the immediate focus on the Ramsey family. The media's intense scrutiny of the Ramseys fueled public speculation, and many outlets prematurely portrayed the Ramseys as guilty. This, in turn, may have pushed investigators to focus more heavily on the family, influencing the direction of their inquiries.

The leak of information to the media also had a significant impact on the investigation. Confidential details, such as the content of the ransom note and specific elements of the crime scene, found their way into media reports. This not only jeopardised the integrity of the investigation but also stirred public speculation and armchair detective work, further complicating the narrative.

The media's role in broadcasting the Ramseys' public appearances and interviews also shaped public opinion. Patsy and John Ramsey's interview with CNN, the press conferences, and later, their book, "The Death of Innocence," allowed the couple to present their side of the story to a broad audience. However, these appearances were also analysed and critiqued, with body language experts and psychologists weighing in on the couple's sincerity, further shaping public perception.

Over time, as the media continued to explore every angle of the case, multiple theories were propagated, including those involving intruders, child beauty pageants, and even Santa Claus impersonators. Such extensive coverage widened the scope of public speculation and fostered a sense of confusion and intrigue that persists to this day.

The JonBenét Ramsey case is a poignant example of how media speculation and biassed reporting can steer a criminal investigation and shape public opinion. It brings to light the power of the media and the ethical considerations necessary in the coverage of such sensitive cases. As we venture further into our exploration of this complex case, the impact of the media remains a crucial element of the narrative that cannot be overlooked.

BEYOND THE HEADLINES: UNRAVELING JONBENÉT RAMSEY

Chapter 8: Echoes of JonBenét: Lessons and Legacy

―――――

The Glitter and the Gloom - Child Beauty Pageants in the Spotlight

JonBenét Ramsey's story brought an unprecedented level of attention to the world of child beauty pageants. Her images, dolled up and looking far older than her tender age, sparked heated discussions about the appropriateness of such events and their potential link to her murder. This chapter will delve into the controversies surrounding child pageants, their relevance to JonBenét's story, and the broader conversation about potential childhood exploitation.

Child beauty pageants were already a contentious subject before JonBenét's case, criticised for sexualizing young girls and promoting harmful beauty standards. JonBenét, a frequent participant in these pageants, became the poster child for this debate following her murder. The media was flooded with photos of her in full makeup, elaborate hairstyles, and glamorous costumes, eliciting both fascination and discomfort. This exposure further fueled concerns about the appropriateness and potential dangers of child pageantry.

The intense scrutiny of JonBenét's participation in pageants also influenced the direction of the investigation. Early suspicions speculated a pageant-obsessed fan or a disgruntled contestant could be the perpetrator, though these theories lost steam as the case progressed. Nonetheless, the association between JonBenét's murder and her involvement in pageants created a sinister undertone that continues to shadow the child pageant industry.

In the years following JonBenét's death, the discourse around child beauty pageants intensified. Advocates for child protection highlighted concerns about the potential for exploitation, the focus on physical beauty, and the stress of competition. Critics argued these pageants encouraged the objectification of young children and questioned their psychological impact.

This controversy has led to significant changes in the child beauty pageant industry. Some states in the U.S. have enforced stricter regulations, and certain countries, like France, have even banned child beauty pageants outright. The industry itself has made efforts to refocus on talent, personality, and age-appropriate presentation.

JonBenét Ramsey's murder remains a tragic, unresolved mystery. Yet, her story has contributed to a significant shift in societal views about child beauty pageants and a greater emphasis on child protection. Her legacy prompts us to question societal norms and encourages us to seek a more compassionate and safe environment for all children.

Lessons Learned - The Impact on Law Enforcement Practices and Investigative Procedures

THE JONBENÉT RAMSEY case, with its high profile nature and subsequent public scrutiny, has had a lasting impact on law enforcement practices and investigative procedures. Mistakes made and lessons learned from this case have led to specific changes in police protocols, particularly in handling similar high-stakes, emotionally charged cases. This chapter will discuss these alterations and their significance.

One of the primary lessons learned from the JonBenét case is the importance of preserving the crime scene. In the initial response to the 911 call from the Ramsey home, the crime scene was not properly secured. Friends and family were allowed in the house, potentially contaminating crucial evidence. This misstep was widely criticised and underscored the vital role a pristine crime scene plays in an investigation. In the wake of this case, law enforcement agencies have placed renewed emphasis on rigorous crime scene preservation and control.

The investigation also brought to light the need for improved communication and cooperation between different law enforcement agencies. The case was marked by discord between the Boulder Police Department and the Boulder County District Attorney's office, contributing to a disjointed investigation. This emphasised the importance of inter-agency collaboration and the need for clear, effective communication channels in high-profile cases.

Further, the handling of media scrutiny in this case led to a reevaluation of how law enforcement agencies engage with the press. The Boulder Police Department faced criticism for leaks of sensitive information, contributing to media frenzy and public speculation. In response, many departments have strengthened their media management strategies, with an emphasis on protecting the integrity of ongoing investigations while maintaining transparency.

Moreover, the case highlighted the necessity for law enforcement to approach family members of victims with a balance of empathy and suspicion. The Ramseys were under intense scrutiny and were subjected to both public and official suspicion, yet the case also made it clear that this suspicion should not lead to tunnel vision that excludes other viable suspects or leads.

Overall, the JonBenét Ramsey case served as a crucial learning opportunity for law enforcement agencies, prompting them to critically evaluate their investigative procedures. The adaptations in response to the case's missteps aim to ensure more effective, nuanced, and balanced investigations in the future.

BEYOND THE HEADLINES: UNRAVELING JONBENÉT RAMSEY

Chapter 9: The Quest for Truth: Current Developments and Cold Case Revisited

———

A New Dawn - Recent Advances in Forensic Technology

The ever-evolving field of forensic science has had a profound influence on criminal investigations, and the JonBenét Ramsey case is no exception. As our technological capabilities continue to expand, the possibilities for breakthroughs in cold cases like JonBenét's increase. This chapter will delve into recent advancements such as DNA analysis, fingerprinting, and other technological breakthroughs that could potentially shed new light on this enduring mystery.

Since the initial investigation into JonBenét's murder, DNA analysis techniques have undergone significant advancements. For instance, the introduction of Next-Generation Sequencing (NGS) provides more detailed and comprehensive DNA profiles than traditional methods. Also, innovations like Touch DNA, a technique that collects and analyses skin cells left behind on an object's surface, could potentially reveal previously unobtainable genetic evidence from the crime scene.

In 2008, this Touch DNA method was applied to JonBenét's clothing and led to the clearing of the Ramsey family members as suspects, as the unknown male DNA found did not match any of theirs. However, with today's even more advanced techniques, including the capacity to potentially determine eye, hair, and skin colour from genetic material, investigators could gain a more detailed picture of the unidentified contributor.

Another area of technological advancement lies in fingerprint analysis. The implementation of Automated Fingerprint Identification Systems (AFIS) has revolutionised the process of matching fingerprints, making it faster and more accurate. If unidentified prints were found at the crime scene, these could be reanalyzed using these more advanced systems, potentially leading to a match that was previously missed.

In addition, newer forensic technologies, such as digital forensics, may provide fresh insights. This encompasses the recovery and analysis of information from digital devices, including computers and smartphones. Although such technology was not prevalent at the time of JonBenét's murder, any existing digital evidence could be reanalyzed with these advanced techniques.

Lastly, the growth of genealogical DNA databases, like those used in the Golden State Killer case, opens new avenues for identifying potential suspects. By comparing crime scene DNA with genetic data available publicly or in law enforcement databases, investigators can potentially find relatives of the unknown DNA contributor and track down the person of interest.

While the use of these advancements has yet to bring resolution to JonBenét's case, they embody a beacon of hope. Each

technological leap strengthens the bridge that could ultimately
lead to the truth, illuminating the path to justice for JonBenét.

Pursuit of Justice - The Renewed Efforts to Solve the Case

THE TRAGIC MYSTERY of JonBenét Ramsey's murder
remains unsolved, but the quest for justice persists. As we step
into the present, it's important to examine the renewed efforts to
solve the case and evaluate the potential for a breakthrough. This
chapter will cover the current state of the investigation and any
notable new leads or developments.

The Boulder Police Department maintains that JonBenét's case
is still open and under active investigation. Over the years, the
department has continually reviewed the case file, retested
evidence using updated forensic techniques, and followed up
on any new leads that emerge. A new team of detectives was
assigned to the case in 2015 to bring fresh eyes to the
investigation and take advantage of advances in forensic
technology.

Key to the renewed efforts is the continued analysis of the DNA
evidence found at the crime scene. The DNA from an unknown
male discovered on JonBenét's clothing is considered to be the
most promising lead. With continued advancements in DNA
analysis techniques, there is hope that this evidence might
eventually provide a definitive link to her killer. Boulder police
have retested this evidence several times over the years, each time
using more advanced techniques in the hope of generating a lead.

Additionally, investigators continue to field tips and leads from the public. In a case that has captivated the national consciousness for so long, the input from the public can be both a help and a hindrance. However, even amidst numerous false leads and unfounded theories, authorities remain vigilant, knowing that a single, solid tip could crack the case wide open.

Furthermore, investigators remain open to the possibility of a confession from the perpetrator. Though this seems unlikely after so many years, it is not unheard of in cold cases. This potential avenue to solving the case underscores the importance of keeping the investigation alive and in the public eye.

In the quest for justice for JonBenét, the value of persistence cannot be understated. While we grapple with the disquieting reality that her killer may never be brought to justice, the continued commitment to solving the case keeps hope alive. The flame of truth may flicker in the winds of time, but it is far from extinguished. As we edge closer to the truth with each passing day, we affirm our unwavering dedication to justice for JonBenét Ramsey.

BEYOND THE HEADLINES: UNRAVELING JONBENÉT RAMSEY

Chapter 10: Forever Remembered: JonBenét's Life and Impact

Celebrating JonBenét: A Tribute to Her Life

In the flurry of mystery, speculation, and controversy surrounding JonBenét Ramsey's untimely death, it is easy to overlook the fact that she was a young girl full of dreams and potential. This chapter aims to honour her life, not as a victim or a tragic figure, but as a vibrant and spirited child. We will explore her interests, achievements, and dreams through anecdotes and stories that reveal her personality and passions.

JonBenét was an exuberant and energetic six-year-old girl who was drawn to the sparkle and glamour of child beauty pageants. She seemed to shine on stage, effortlessly captivating audiences with her infectious smile and outgoing personality. Yet, behind the sparkling tiaras and flashy costumes was a girl who enjoyed simple childhood pleasures like playing with her friends or riding her bike around the neighbourhood.

JonBenét's mother, Patsy, would often recount stories of her daughter's vivacious spirit and how she loved to perform. One such story was JonBenét's love for playing the piano. Even though she was only in kindergarten, she had begun taking piano lessons. Despite her small hands barely spanning the keys, she would eagerly try to follow along with her piano teacher, demonstrating a curiosity and determination that was indicative of her character.

Her older brother, Burke, often spoke about their playful sibling rivalry and their shared adventures. JonBenét was not just a beauty queen, but a little sister who enjoyed teasing her brother and engaging in typical sibling mischief. Despite the nine-year age gap, Burke and JonBenét were close, often playing games together, with JonBenét's competitive spirit frequently coming to the fore.

JonBenét also harboured dreams of following in her mother's footsteps by becoming Miss America one day. Even at such a tender age, she showed a fascination for the world beyond her home in Boulder, Colorado. She was drawn to the idea of representing her country and was inspired by the poise and grace of the Miss America contestants she saw on television.

Yet beyond her dreams of pageantry, JonBenét was, at her core, a regular child with a love for animals and outdoor adventures. One of her dreams was to own a pony, showcasing a tender side that resonated with many children her age.

It is important to remember JonBenét in this way - as a vibrant, lively child with dreams and a zest for life. While we continue to seek justice for her tragic death, let us not forget to celebrate her life, cherishing the joy and light she brought into the world during her brief time here.

Legacy of Loss: Symbolic Significance of JonBenét Ramsey

THE STORY OF JONBENÉT Ramsey transcends the tragic narrative of her unsolved murder. In the wake of her untimely death, a legacy has emerged that continues to impact society in profound ways. JonBenét Ramsey, in her short, vibrant life and the mystery surrounding her death, has become a potent symbol of lost innocence and unresolved justice.

In the public consciousness, JonBenét represents the lost innocence of childhood. Her image — the cherubic six-year-old girl with sparkling eyes, dressed in pageant gowns and crowns — is a stark contrast to the grim reality of her fate. It's a heartbreaking juxtaposition that hits at the core of our collective fears for the safety of our own children and the harsh realities that can shatter their innocence. This emotional resonance contributes significantly to our continued fascination and emotional investment in her story.

At the same time, JonBenét's unsolved murder epitomises the haunting spectre of unresolved justice. Her case has become a symbol of the countless cold cases that remain unsolved, each one a testament to the painful reality that justice is not always served. The inability to solve her murder despite the passage of so many years and the use of advanced investigative methods is a sobering reminder of the fallibility of our justice system. It fuels a persistent demand for truth, a resolution that allows for closure and justice not only for JonBenét but also for other victims of unsolved crimes.

Furthermore, the media frenzy and public fascination surrounding JonBenét's case have provoked significant reflection and critique of our societal obsession with true crime. It calls into question the fine line between seeking justice and exploiting tragedy for entertainment. This, too, is part of her legacy — a reminder of our responsibility to approach such sensitive topics with respect and integrity.

The enduring legacy of JonBenét Ramsey also extends to her impact on child beauty pageants, discussions around childhood exploitation, and the reform of investigative procedures in cases involving child victims. Her case has undoubtedly sparked changes and heightened awareness in these areas.

While the circumstances of JonBenét's death are tragic and her murder remains unresolved, her enduring impact on society continues to resonate. Her story serves as a reminder of the fragility of innocence, the quest for justice, and the societal responsibility we bear when engaging with true crime narratives. As we strive for justice for JonBenét, we also work towards a more conscious, empathetic society, ensuring her legacy is not in vain.

BEYOND THE HEADLINES: UNRAVELING JONBENÉT RAMSEY

Epilogue: Seeking Closure

―――

Lingering Questions: Unanswered Questions

Despite the passage of time, the intense scrutiny, and the tireless efforts of many, the murder of JonBenét Ramsey remains one of the most perplexing unsolved cases in American history. A fog of unanswered questions and unresolved aspects still shrouds the events of December 26th, 1996. As we near the end of our exploration, it is crucial to revisit these lingering questions, and invite readers to ponder, reflect, and perhaps envision potential resolutions.

The first unanswered question is the one that sits at the heart of the case: Who killed JonBenét Ramsey? Was it an intruder who found his way into the Ramsey home? Was it a member of the family? Despite numerous theories and suspects, we still do not have a definitive answer. DNA evidence found on JonBenét's clothing suggests an unknown male was present, but this evidence has yet to conclusively point to a perpetrator.

The second question is tied to the peculiar ransom note found in the Ramsey's house. Who wrote it? And why was it left behind despite JonBenét's body being found in the basement? The lengthy and unusual ransom note, apparently written using a pen and pad from the Ramsey home, has been a key point of intrigue. Analysis of the note has led to conflicting opinions, but no conclusive attribution has been made.

A third unresolved aspect is the precise cause and time of JonBenét's death. The autopsy report showed she had suffered a blow to the head and had been strangled, but it was not clear which came first or how much time passed between these events. The timing of these events could potentially shed more light on whether her death was a result of a deliberate act or a tragic accident followed by a cover-up.

Further unresolved questions pertain to the presence of an intruder. If it was an intruder, how did they enter and leave the house without leaving more evidence or waking anyone? Why would an intruder spend time writing a ransom note inside the house, rather than bringing one with them? If it was not an intruder, how do we account for the unknown DNA found at the crime scene?

As we ponder these questions and the many others that remain, we must confront the unsettling possibility that we may never know exactly what happened to JonBenét Ramsey. Yet, in the pursuit of justice and truth, it is our duty to continue questioning, examining, and searching for answers.

As we conclude our exploration, we invite you, the reader, to join in this quest for resolution. Reflect upon the evidence, the theories, and the lingering questions. Who do you believe is responsible, and why? As you turn the final pages of this book, you join a collective consciousness grappling with a tragedy that has touched many lives, and your reflections contribute to the ongoing quest for justice and understanding.

The Quest for Closure - The Importance of Resolving High-Profile Cases

CLOSURE IS A CRITICAL part of the healing process for victims and their families. It provides a sense of finality, allowing those affected to move forward in their grief. However, in high-profile, unresolved cases like JonBenét Ramsey's, closure extends beyond the immediate circle of those directly affected. It bears significance for the community at large, the justice system, and our collective societal consciousness.

For the Ramsey family, closure would mean an end to their decades-long battle to find JonBenét's killer and clear their name from the swirl of suspicion that has surrounded them. The resolution of the case would allow them to finally mourn their daughter's death without the constant intrusion of speculation and media frenzy. It would also be a vindication of their insistence on their innocence.

From a broader perspective, the resolution of JonBenét's case is important to the community of Boulder, Colorado, where the crime occurred. An unresolved child murder case shakes the foundation of safety and security within a community, creating a lingering fear and suspicion. Closure can help restore faith in the community's ability to protect its members and offer some measure of peace to those who still remember the shocking crime.

For the justice system, solving this case is a matter of institutional integrity and credibility. The initial mishandling of the case, the procedural errors, and the inability to provide answers have been a blight on the reputation of the Boulder Police Department and the district attorney's office. Finding JonBenét's killer would not only restore faith in these institutions but also offer learnings to prevent such missteps in future cases.

Furthermore, resolving high-profile cases such as JonBenét's helps to maintain public trust in the justice system. Unsolved cases, particularly those that attract as much public attention as JonBenét's, can fuel scepticism about the effectiveness of law enforcement and the judicial process. Closure reassures the public that justice can, and will, be served, no matter how complex or high-profile the case.

On a societal level, the narrative of unresolved justice, epitomised by JonBenét's case, contributes to a broader discourse about justice, victimhood, and the media's role in shaping these narratives. Resolution can stimulate conversations about improving these dynamics, impacting how we engage with true crime narratives.

In essence, closure is not just about finding JonBenét's killer; it's about healing a community, restoring faith in the justice system, and stimulating societal growth. As we continue to seek the truth about what happened to JonBenét, we carry with us the hope that one day we will find these much-needed resolutions.

As we close this exploration into the enigmatic and heart-wrenching case of JonBenét Ramsey, it is clear that her story extends far beyond the confines of a cold case file. It's a story that has evolved into a complex tapestry of societal critique, familial tragedy, and a quest for justice that has spanned decades.

"Beyond the Headlines: Unravelling JonBenét Ramsey" has not been merely a retelling of the events that occurred on December 26, 1996. Instead, it has been an invitation to engage deeply with the multifaceted narrative surrounding JonBenét's life and death. While we may never uncover the full truth of what happened to JonBenét, it is my hope that this book has brought us closer to understanding the broader implications of her story, fostering empathy, critical thought, and a shared commitment to seeking justice.

It is a testament to the enduring legacy of a six-year-old girl named JonBenét, who, in both her life and her untimely death, continues to touch the hearts of millions around the world. As we turn the final page, let us carry forward the lessons learned and keep alive the quest for truth and justice in her memory.

Don't miss out!

Visit the website below and you can sign up to receive emails whenever Will Anderson publishes a new book. There's no charge and no obligation.

https://books2read.com/r/B-A-TYIZ-WYKLC

BOOKS 2 READ

Connecting independent readers to independent writers.

Also by Will Anderson

About the Author

Will Anderson is a highly acclaimed author specializing in true crime. His captivating storytelling delves into the dark world of serial killers and unsolved criminal mysteries. The "Behind the Mask" series, his most notable work, peels back the layers of well-known killers, offering an in-depth examination of their twisted minds. Anderson's meticulous research and psychological insights create a gripping reading experience. With an unwavering commitment to truth and justice, he sheds light on cold cases, giving a voice to victims and closure to their families. Will Anderson's contributions to the true crime genre have solidified his place as a respected and sought-after author.

* 9 7 9 8 2 2 3 7 8 5 5 6 9 *